Clara's
Better-than-Okay
Day

Story by Janeen Brian
Illustrations by JiaJia Hamner

Clara's Better-than-Okay Day

Text: Janeen Brian
Publishers: Tania Mazzeo and Eliza Webb
Series consultant: Amanda Sutera
  Hands on Heads Consulting
Editor: Jarrah Moore
Project editor: Annabel Smith
Designer: Jess Kelly
Project designer: Danielle Maccarone
Illustrations: JiaJia Hamner
Production controller: Renee Tome

NovaStar

ISBN 978 0 17 033423 5

Cengage Learning Australia
Level 5, 80 Dorcas Street
Southbank VIC 3006 Australia
Phone: 1300 790 853
Email: aust.nelsonprimary@cengage.com

For learning solutions, visit **cengage.com.au**

Printed in China by 1010 Printing International Ltd
1 2 3 4 5 6 7 28 27 26 25 24

*Nelson acknowledges the Traditional Owners and Custodian
of the lands of all First Nations Peoples. We pay respect
to Elders past and present, and extend that respect to
all First Nations Peoples today.*

Contents

MONDAY

TUESDA'

Chapter 1

The New Teacher

Clara scrambled out of bed and ran her finger along the daily timetable above her desk.

"Mum! It's Tuesday!" Clara rushed into the kitchen, tapping her fingertips together in alarm.

Her mother was busy preparing breakfast. She turned to Clara and said, "It'll be all right, love."

"It won't be! The new teacher is starting today. I don't want a new teacher. I only want Ms Dayman."

Clara's mother sighed. "Ms Dayman's having a baby, Clara. We've talked about this before. And the new teacher, Mr Adams, knows you have autism."

Clara twisted her mouth. "Of course he'd know." Her voice rose. "Because I'm the only one in the class who has it."

"Come on, love. Take some deep breaths."

Clara turned away. "I need Ribbee!"

Clara sat tight in the car, making a low humming noise. She squeezed her special squishy toy frog, Ribbee. Ribbee calmed her down.

But at the classroom doorway, Clara froze. Then Mrs Shen appeared and beckoned. Mrs Shen was the extra teacher who helped Clara with her work.

"Morning," Mrs Shen said gently.

"Morning, Mrs Shen," said Clara's mum. "Clara, I have to go now. Everything will be fine, love. I'll see you this afternoon."

"But, Mum –" Clara stammered.

Mrs Shen quickly ushered Clara inside.

The new teacher greeted Clara with a warm smile and said, "I see you have a toy frog. That's interesting."

Mr Adams didn't say why Ribbee was interesting. And Clara didn't ask.

In fact, Clara was too busy looking around the classroom. It was wrong. Different.

Clara's eyes darted here and there. All the tables had been moved around. Unusual posters were on the walls. There was something big and covered up on Mr Adams's desk. Clara clutched Ribbee to her chest.

And where was Aster? Her friend should be here by now. Clara's breaths came in short puffs.

Mrs Shen pointed to the Reading Corner. "Look, that's the same, Clara. And the cushions. And the frog books are on the shelves."

Clara kept clutching Ribbee tightly. Aster still wasn't here. What if she didn't come today? It was too much to think about. Clara began to jiggle.

"Hi, Clara!"

Clara knew that voice. "Aster! Where have you been?"

"Hello to you, too, Clara." Aster chuckled.
"I had to go to the dentist before school.
I got a filling. See?" She opened her mouth.
Clara peered in, then turned away.

"Are you okay?" Aster asked.

Clara pressed her lips together and nodded
towards Mr Adams.

"It'll be all right," said Aster. "He hasn't got
two heads!"

Clara frowned. "Of course not. He wouldn't
be teaching if he had two heads."

Aster grinned. "Let's sit down."

Chapter 2

It's All Different

Clara sat with her elbows on the table and her hands cupped near her ears in case Mr Adams was a loud teacher. He wasn't. Then she held her arms and legs in close in case he rushed about the classroom. He didn't. And his shirt wasn't so bright that it hurt her head.

Mr Adams started talking about their excursion to the Gorge Wildlife Park the following day, and how there'd be a special guest speaker. The whole class sat up, eyes bright.

But Clara shrank back in her chair. She liked animals, but the rest of the information was too much to remember. She wrapped her fingers around Ribbee and began to squeeze.

Then Mr Adams pointed to the hidden object on his desk.

"Who'd like to guess what's under the cover?" he asked.

Hands shot up.

"A meteorite!"

"A baby elephant!"

"Your lunch!"

The class laughed.

Mr Adams lifted the cover.

Clara glanced at it. She gasped.

It was a terrarium with two tree frogs, one squatting on a branch. Mr Adams said that the frogs would stay here while the class was learning about Australian animals.

Clara's toes tingled. Next thing, she was at the front, staring into the terrarium.

"Mr Adams," said Aster, "Clara knows a lot about frogs."

"Yes, I do," said Clara. "For example, in captivity, tree frogs can live up to 20 years. That's old. But it's because they don't have predators. I've seen every one of Gary Tyler's online videos. I watch them all the time! He's the Frog Whisperer and my hero."

The class clapped.

"Thank you, Clara," said Mr Adams, as Clara sat down. "Now do you see why I mentioned your frog when you arrived?" He smiled. "Okay, everyone. Thinking caps on. We'll have to come up with some names for our frogs."

Clara bit her lip with excitement. The frogs would be staying in the classroom for a while, so she could see them every day.

After lunch, Clara and Aster lay on the cushions in the Reading Corner. Aster read Clara a frog book three times. Clara was feeling better about the day.

Chapter 3

Ribbee Comes, Too

But when Clara checked her timetable
the next morning, her insides became
hot and fluttery. It was the day of the
excursion. She was nervous about the bus
trip. And she'd never been to that wildlife
park before – she didn't know what would
happen. Clara moaned and wrung her
hands. But Aster was going, and Clara
wanted to be with her friend.

Finally, she swung her backpack onto
her shoulder.

"You've got your lunch?" asked her mum.
"And Ribbee?"

Clara nodded.

"Don't get them mixed up, will you?"
Her mum grinned.

Clara glared. "Mum, as if I'd eat Ribbee instead of my lunch."

On the bus, Clara and Aster sat together. Mrs Shen was close by. Clara stared straight ahead. She wouldn't look out the window. Or play "I Spy" with Aster. Instead, she clutched Ribbee and hummed.

Once they were out of the bus, Clara stuck close to Aster while a park ranger welcomed them.

Then, Mr Adams said, "It's time to start exploring. Take your water bottles, notepads and pens. We have tablets for those who want to take photos." He waved a bright yellow flag. "As long as you can still see this, you can wander the park in pairs."

"This will be great!" said Aster. "Let's go and see the kangaroos in the paddock first. There's a joey."

"I'm taking Ribbee," said Clara.

Chapter 4

Lost

Clara walked slowly. Sometimes she scrunched up her nose at the strange smells. She gazed at a peacock spreading its feathers and at an alligator sliding into a pool. The screeches from cockatoos startled her, and she clutched Ribbee.

After lunch, Clara suddenly shrieked in panic. "Ribbee!" she cried. "Where is he?"

She spun in a circle, eyes flashing, mouth open in horror. "I've lost Ribbee!"

"I'll help you find him," said Aster.

But at that very moment, Mr Adams called everyone over.

"Come on, class," he said. "Time for our guest speaker."

"No!" Clara waved her arms in distress. "Ribbee's lost! Ribbee's lost!"

"It's okay, Clara," said Mrs Shen. "I'll find him."

"No! I need to!" cried Clara, and she began to run.

"Clara!" said Mrs Shen, speeding up. "Why don't you go and see who the guest speaker is? I'll find Ribbee. I promise. Look, Aster's waving. She's saved a seat for you."

Clara jiggled and shook her head, but Aster was pointing excitedly to a man nearby. Clara took a few steps and paused. Then she gave a yelp of surprise.

"It's Gary Tyler!"

Chapter 5

We're the Same!

Gary Tyler, the Frog Whisperer, smiled as Clara rushed up to her seat.

"Just in time," he said in a kind voice. "I have some fabulous frogs to show you all today."

"Yay!" cried Clara. But her insides were shuddering and she kept looking over her shoulder. Ribbee was still missing.

After a few long minutes, Mrs Shen arrived. "Found him," she said.

Clara took the toy frog, thanked Mrs Shen and quickly began to squeeze Ribbee.

Gary Tyler looked at Clara. "Is that a special squishy toy?" he asked.

Startled, Clara looked down for a moment and then nodded.

The Frog Whisperer pushed his hat to the back of his head. "I had one of those toys when I was a kid. Mine was a dog. It helped calm me down. You know why I needed him?" He paused. "Because I have autism."

Clara's breath halted in her throat.

"I have autism, too!" Her voice rose in shock. She was the same as her hero. And he was the same as her! Grinning, Clara waved her toy frog. "And this is Ribbee!" she cried.

Back at school, everyone agreed it had been a great day.

Especially Clara.

"Even Ribbee got to meet Gary Tyler," she said.

Aster giggled.

"Before we go home," said Mr Adams, "it's time we gave our two frogs some names. Did you put your thinking caps on?"

The class voted "Taddy" for the male frog.

"And for the female frog?" said Mr Adams.

"I reckon it should be 'Clara'," said Aster.

"Yeah!" cried the class. "Clara!"

Clara's insides suddenly felt warm and happy. She stood and bowed.

"Thank you, everybody," she said.

Today had been a better-than-okay day. In fact, it had been the best day ever!